The Answer Lies Beneath The Ink

THE ANSWER LIES BENEATH THE INK

First edition. November 16, 2024.

ISBN: 979-8230578420

Written by Clark West Cooper.

Written By

Clark West Cooper

The Healing Chronicles

I

Intro

"Straight Jacket Free"

When it is time, when there is no more room for mistake. We treasure all we can musk, gathering the grapes from poorly standing vines. In love I feel a way. Through righteousness I know this pain will fade. With a coursing curse I feel your kiss will forever take my breath away. Existing stories that help bleed my soul free of shame, I know someday I will find my place.

...

We can accept existence or ignore the main frame. To see through the horizon and believe again. We view this slumber as a steep hill. Hold tight, be close through this travel through the mind, holding and counting upon the rosary beaded necklace that is hung around. I travel through what is hidden. I found the secret and I am sharing this with you. A love that is so pure we forget to remember the other stories, we believe that we are one and happy, so let us not ignore and live through a metaphor shaped halo of beauty through reflection.

...

"Wonder only to ponder through imagination."

...

Crashing waves enter a disturbed mind. We have become over cumbered with our troubles and ignore in self and others close. To stare upon the fortress of beautiful eyes, we refrain from the jacket-less curse to be overly cold.

Shaped into a metaphor with no understanding we shed our tears in a prayer soaked dream to be forgiven and to walk our path once more with head held high upon the crowns we so choose to believe. Crazed and dazed into the confusion of self-inner thought. Let us follow the heart that beats as our own and travel our road as someone new, the one you have always dreamed to be.

...

"The brand new You, The brand new Me."

Phase One
"The Fear Inside A broken Mind"
...
A shade in discomfort, another word to value within the bliss of virtue
Only to dream to wake in your arms, when fear has taken hold of where charm once lived so freely
A world so cold, a place to wish away, such fear to endure, as it takes away each waking breath and hovers like a halo above my reflection
Feeling dead deep down within the basement of my spirit, where feelings arise in the coldness of the newly awoken lonesomeness that within dwells the fear of never succeeding on letting go of the past
Left to shed beneath the only standing willow tree of faded dreams and regretful memories
Lost in wonder of who I am and who I must become

...

Torn between cupped hands, begging for forgiveness and caressing in higher tides that crash ashore as I watch in still motion as they wash away everything I have ever once loved

...

Shredding pages of the lost art that has become my passion, forgotten words left to rot upon the forbidden bookshelf

...

Only a tragedy to view through such a perspective where I can only grow without faith, hope and love for you
To forever dream of and share the scenery of the beauty beyond what the eye can see

...

To cherish oneself in a distant and soothing form of calming harmony in which we sing and praise in belief from deep within

...

A belief of such purity that most can never dare to ask to feel, such a wonder in such a small view, even through a microscope, the elements of feelings to adore can only be felt, but never to be seen even through the sharpest sight, only in a dream can the feel be so curious only to act as real as real can only feel

...

The greatest sensation to cover the world in grace, to retrace each step and retake without fear, only in that case of satisfaction, can I ever decide on what to make right and what to leave behind.

"The Fear That Grew Within A Tame And Withering Soul Set To Forgive"
I cast into the shadows whisper, a calm and soothing notion to the oceans waves that crash ashore
Allowing me to breathe and see once more

...

Shaken to torment, cuddled in a hole filled blanket, weeping under the moon, what a silhouette, I must be deep beneath the sea in direst and haunted screams that are filling my conscious with suspicion of myself, to be the one denied of my own dreams even with the will and strength needed to succeed and the unquestionable ability to reach any dream that shines so vividly and bright, it is hard to stare into because it is blinding to the eyes yet, so adoring I cannot stop myself but to look and attempt to see into the future that I am creating by building my own destiny

...

Church yard bells are ringing in my ears, fulfilled and in still motion to the oceans currents and sky blotting wishes
I can scream each day of the fear that grows within
Why say it all with just a pen, instead I add a way to read this in harmony

...

When I was cold and oh so shallow, others just could never understand, my way of wasting away every second of every day, while still holding onto something worth more than gold, my heart, my soul and my passion

...

They say to dream it out, while the voices said to capture and forever hold

Stuck in-between shades that ignore and are stunningly brightly lit, only shades that are lonely and reach of another attempt to ignore yet, this time a bit more

...

Fantasy to dreams, my faded eyes are as red as the blood you have seen

Crafted then casted so well, it must have flew a hundred yards, within treasure and metal it was built, to frame the picture that was painted once more

To view what I have seen is only an artist that never could, but in faith always will, and one day will prove that impossible is only a word for defeating your own dream and ignoring your own voice that is screaming within

...

A wish upon the reality, a distraction in its finest that learns how to comprehend

...

Shouting where only wolfs sing, burning in ditches, within each scratch to the itch it hobbles and sways

Follow me now the voice demands, what am I thinking of, well... I can't fully explain

The details are blurry, the whispers so soft, a glimpse of the future I sought, only to view the legacy I was to bring and leave behind to forever capture the beauty behind each work of art

Why continue on, as each phrase causes tears, I begin to fall down only to cry out the loneliness I felt, always as I was left to be alone, in self-imprisoned shame and in guilt, while crowded with the sense of knowingly doubt

...

To the day where I began to think about strength and to the odd mission

While it was beauty I felt and watched as it slowly began to fade away

Only a dream, only to the song it sings, only to believe so purely, can you even begin to seek

"Is It Crazy or Just Simply Insanity...Brilliance As A Picture, Within Such Wondrous Thought, Portrayed So Eloquently."

...

My thoughts trigger the sting and force the terror in which you scream, words that shout, screaming of fear yet, only to be portrayed so beautifully

...

If capture is happiness as its key, why am I forced to be known as the last one to seek, when surely you know, I must be the first, for failure is not an option and what is hand to hand, only the pure and its passion splattered upon each wall you cross

For within me I fear there is a demon beside me, even though I feel as if I'm guided by the angels

Not coincidental, for facts are a straight line and liars are the curved minds

...

"Turn it forward, roll the carpet...ouch."

I'm screaming at air wishing for more as oxygen must be something I have held to know it is real

To be the frame instead of the picture, I must be in doubt for that's being a forgetful thinker, if you call it a rhyme than that is a remedy that can fill its wasted time

If you can capture the words to call the guards, bring in a country and portray what is sanity

Only to the insane that is never tamed, forgotten and scarred as to a dismissal of a zero card

Labeled as insane but brilliant to its people

...

Now that the thought has sat down with me, I was able to discuss the wolf I created, in personal and descriptive ways I cried my pages to the elephant, who seemed like the giraffe to discard of the matter

...

If my words don't mean a thing to you, then I praise in a god I wish I could only know, lord you promised in glamor and gold they would worship your words that speak through me, some kind of way of creative and imaginative originality, bring me the courage to wish to exist so I can put this shame to rest and finally just live

By now the tears have dried as I write to you with teary eyes, in a wishful way, I thank you for more, only in practice may I capture this stride, only to be practically alive, such as water poured into a glass to be turned into wine

Inside a prayer that was brought back by the dreams of a penny, dark as my head boats, only one that can swim in noon, so the wolf and I cried at the site of these words, only in a higher promise may my voice sing before your eyes

...

After the tears have dried, I write to you in teary eyes, in question of "Is It Crazy or Just Simply Insanity...Brilliance As A Picture yet, How Can One Portray Such Words So Eloquently?"

...

Without mistake we may never understand why right is always for the best, when wrong is to put to rest

while I starve, I try to eat the ocean and caress in her waves to adore, along the journey I found something infinitely interesting

To cross this squiggly line into the devotion, into the transmission I
have flown straight through, once before the Lord
In beauty and detriment

...

"Follow me," he then said, into the abyss of what wanders beyond the
gloom from the shine of the sun and the moon, crossing eyes into
rosary beads, the only eyes we truly can never see
Breathing very slowly as I look into your eyes and you watch as I drift
away
I finish my time here with my last words

...

"I have lived in this world for what seems eternity, living in fear and
afraid to take the next step, I regret all of my choices and can only
dream and wish upon another chance to relive my past, change the
choices I had made to correct each fault in each of my steps."

"The Secret Of The Buried Charm Within Existence A Star We Forever Dreamt Upon"
After the passage into another time and space where my spirit drifts alone
I am seeking revenge on behalf of myself
Take a razor, no not good enough, does anyone have a better way besides self-harm?

...

What about triumph and acceptance, to relive is not my darkened corner, between each moment as I flew into another zone, I am relieved with a sense that this is so beautifully expressed
To describe what I have seen, you would only hear to never comprehend
For words have no meaning to describe this unknown feeling
Without a world so cold, I would not be here now, to view a form of color and brightness so vividly is to only dream of such a fantasy

...

I bled into liquid as the whispers fade, which arrive my thoughts to guilty of the innocence while I was left alone in a world so cold
As I drowned beneath fear, no one was there to help and to pull me up away from the storm
As the torment considered me as daring, it was simply over at that moment, screaming out to me, "I won't allow anyone to live the life that you were meant to live, so the demons came to shine upon your existence, just to fade you into a mind state of causing no less than severe harm to yourself and everyone else to anything you have ever loved."

...

Within that storm I raged into belief and into pure belief, I'm ready to fight

Bring the angels of my soul, whisper ambition, speak of your wisdom and guide me through this troubled channel, I'm tired of drowning and I wish to suffocate no more

Then the wind flew passed to fight against my fear just to show it that I have had enough, sick and tired, I'm standing once again on my feet just to forget everything. "Positivity!" I scream allowed just to shy away the phantom, in a belief that held the answer to solve the darkest of riddles I was to answer for everyone else, including myself

...

In my secret tale, lies the image of reflection, the answer to life

Question to debate, within the choice I made, to soar high above in search of reach to the star I always dreamed to hold and to grasp the concept upon life itself, a secret buried too deep to dig upon the capture of its meaning and reason for its existence to ponder about within the haze of a lost charm.

"A Meaningless Life Grew Into Beauty As Life Answered The Lost Riddles Of Time"

Praise the acceptance, follow your heart, and trust yourself to believe in yourself

In the end you will find a smile upon your face and then I wouldn't have to watch you as you drift away

...

Within the karma safe from the corner, I stood my ground which pleased the Maker, away from the bottom, along with no more past to dwell upon

...

I followed the light as the house carpenter asked me to come along

To join him on a walk on some distant shore line, the edge of humanity deep within the spirit form

...

As he spoke about the answers to all unanswered questions, he spoke these calming words to me in a soft whisper, "There is beauty that we can see to answer the riddles, a form of such view that we are unable to comprehend yet, the answer to every riddle of life, lives and breathes inside of each beautiful sight we see and yearn to view, to truly find what you seek within your questions to the riddles of life, you must look deep enough within yourself to solve. The Lost Riddles Of Time."

...

I was in such shock but only to not feel anything but pure happiness and relief, something identified as another loving their soul mate, love and trust beneath every word we speak, to every decision we face, beautiful in thought and the conquer of our fears, a form of life never heard and one that never shows its face yet, never has the need to disappear

...

As I spoke of such a world, I began to feel the treasure of gold within, the view, the feeling, the bond between the Maker and I, something to forever cherish and to hold in certainty

...

"Life is no longer meaningless,
it is filled with passion and curiosity for every thought that passes through my vision,
a state of mind where nothing can cause harm or detachment from myself, between the hollow in my eyes,
I once feared it would eat me up inside, now that I have found my reason to keep on breathing for all of the others, the weak, the wounded, the sad and broken lonely spirits that drift into the darkness of the atmosphere,

I speak upon words of beauty to heal your wounds and forgive you of your sins and to dry your eyes that cry tears of pure beauty, to wash away the filth that covers you,

while with a touch of cleanliness you can now begin once again, truly live and to be who you have always wished to be, finally, to chase those stars that shine for only you, to fulfill your own destiny and give rebirth to yourself without ever again feeling the fear that once sheltered you from within."

"Only Truth Stands Still In The Harmony In Each Song We Have Sung"
Tragedy between the beads of sweat dripping off my saddened grin
To smile is not a wish, only to exist is what I miss
Call it insane or brilliance, whatever it may be, it feels as cold as death itself, yet beautiful words in such gorgeous works of art lead me to feel more alive than I have ever felt before, in this life or any past life my spirit has ever had to endure
Never through a naked eye have you seen the perspective of reality and the consciousness of a single glorious thought that no one has ever thought before, a concept we think only to forget and to ignore
...
Captured then withdrew, army to have, army to not, hardly blown from the tops of the gloom
Smiling in the face of death that stares back into my poor reflection that you wish you saw, when the time comes for me to take my leave, I will leave in a state of full gratitude
...
As hours pass I sit to relax, only to ponder on what exist at all, for what exist if we must not, to notice everything exist far beyond what the eye can see
To mistake my view, only to forget to comprehend, show me a single mind capable of these thoughts that exist to never drown below an answer to the conscious of mine
Selective in baring forgotten dreams left to rot, upon the bookshelf of the brilliance between the letters for whom created me, and which maker created you, what God left us to never comprehend or to ever understand
...

Take me upon flight with stars gleaming of tears crying beauty for me as angels sing and fight to protect my existence, until I have reached out to the world in hope and wonder that you can now understand my ways and the purpose in which I speak in this form of language or tongue so to speak

...

Why cower beneath the door, a shelf to bang my head against, when the thoughts begin to overwhelm

Genius is the price of illness at its finest, only to dream upon another story to dwell before this one is gone, but not too late to forget to remember what miracle this has brought upon

To face this fear I will travel this earth, from stone to stone and brick to brick, I will cast out my will and reel in the life I always wished upon a star to live

...

To grasp the concept of the brilliance behind each single thought, which screams of a whisper to create a difference within each of us, a new look into this mad world as we roam lost in its craze that we live only to gather its praise and continue to live

...

Fear grows within the capture of my new perspective, only a miracle can enter and devour the attack of evil against my own strength and courage

Demons that scream and shout beneath the heaven we praise as the stars glisten above the velvet night sky, we hold hands and gather around the flowing stream of the matter of life

To sing our saddened tales that shout of our resilience to endure anymore pain and fear to whomever may bring, it is our time to fight for our own world and our right of peace and understanding in such a callous world, where every thought seems wrong, yet only the truth is in each tale we have sung to every fading memory we lived through along with our desire to protect our inner dreams and search to seek what we wish to find buried deep within the soil of time, footprints faded, yet this mystery is mine.

"The Choice To Reach Is To Be Beautiful And Fulfilled Within Your Own Life"
To dream to never wake, a sad day within my own awakening wish to arouse others by my confession of self-imprisoned intelligence that wakes to all white, violent screams and bloodshot eyes within complete accidental access, when only words are fueled devices and when I speak of the words
"I love you."
I finish with a simple yet, poetic phrase of
"I truly do."
...

Back in her arms I lay and cry, in relief and in complete surprise of what is to come and to pass into the abyss of forgotten lies
...

My pulse begins to pound faster and harder than it has ever before, a scare and shiver sent through what exist to only be adored, a curved spine left to dangle by the root in which it clings to, its placement in order to keep you in tact yet, with a slight curve it can permanently shape you in discomfort, while you shed your tears in your own lonesome fear of what is beneath your confidence of self that hides beneath the surface of what is able to be seen as your outer image, paying no such attention to how truly beautiful you really are
...

To survive is a wish that I believe in, something to keep me moving mountains after climbing each one, reaching the top and shouting as a mountaineer

"My Maker, I have done it, I carried myself this far, no matter what obstacle I come across, I will never fear or show weakness again, I will stand my ground and show my passion to defeat the demons that shade each storm and try to torment my insides with hatred for no one other than myself."

...

To show what hails down, to break the ground that our holy statue has walked upon

A running start to reach the end before I fail and fall before the failure of another's hand

To evaporate what is in sight of your eyes, to regurgitate what has held you back from taking a forward step into your future life

...

To speak as my voice can protest every wrong that we commit and ask for forgiveness, just to commit the same action and repeat the process as if it were a form of positive repetition

A self-drawn memory in existence that fades as a whisper is pulled back from your perfect circle

A never ending form of evolution, we seek for answers only to find our questions are to last forever, deep within the wonder that we ponder within a mind created in pure genius and beyond the most beautiful design

...

To say how long it has been since I have felt sorry, it has been a long time since I have feared for my own self through actions and decisions I have made

...

I continue to carry on in the manner of which I will not fear and show no remorse for my own sin, for within my choice before it is made and acted upon, I make it clear and always make sure for in this step forward I will hold no future regret to any consequence that I would have to render

...

To inspire you through unspoken tales of this world, as wind acts as a cheating sin, as conspiring tidal waves crash the shore and destroy anything that it comes across, such disaster within mother nature, another sad and destructive tale to speak to another

...

What wicked ways to fall before death, what a disgrace for which disaster may come next

...

"A new perspective comes along only to share the realization, that with each moment we take a breath, to every moment that takes our breath away, we are to cherish the life we were given in order to seek pure happiness from within cold and trembling hearts,
which speaks of pure words that have forever since the dawn of man changed the choice and belief in another, a miracle shown before the dawn of rebirth to another in the hands of pity, another card to be dealt along with one more attempt to heal themselves with the help from one who seeks to mend, in wish and prayer the need to help a wounded soul is to never disappear and within confidence and passion those who seek to reach into the wounded never fade into the darkness yet, to spread more than truth behind our existence and each of our purposes, with the secret meaning behind the signs that cause a never ending sense of wondering."

...

To be so purely beautiful is not what we see, it is what makes us who
we are on the inside
A person is who they are and who they make themselves to be, a
dream to fulfill or a dream to never succeed

...

The choice is yours to decide to conquer your wildest dreams or to
never attempt and live with the regret of unhappiness, while asking
for eternity the simple and most popular question
Of
"What If?"

"The Apathy Of Existence Of Holding No Product Of Fear"
To discover myself wanting, waiting for more than curiosity, a dream
fulfilled while being neglected
A boy rides on his bike, as he passes my ashes fall beneath the words
once said, as photographs half-forgotten through movement and
time lay under the bed

...

Feeling safe inside, under the cabinet, a kiss that has burned me yet, I
was always returning
Such an impression of myself, what lies as not much to conceal
To say much to nothing, laughing to the feel that drives insanity up
the walls, only to cure the ill
Pure and soothing, calm to the sway of motion, creating a crescent in
shape, that dawns upon each new waking day

...

Dream to carry no fear, as fear is only a product of our imagination,
you do have the power to rid the existence of fear
Fear is not real, it only exist within the thoughts of our future

Stray to ride, stride to conceal and to rid this disease of our consciousness
A knock at the door shakes and shivers, bored inside yet, I can't switch beneath what holds no switch
…
Take what is the source of what scares you
And
Tempt the notion to pass beyond what is lack of sleep and electricity
…
No fear, no ill, nothing is real, except what I make real during my existence and time here on our planet Earth

Phase Two
"A Lost Riddle In Actual Belief Of A Once Existing Love"
...
I have felt the touch of beauty, I have caressed within the oceans waves
The oldest form of beauty as we know of today

...
To close your eyes and let me touch you now, the only wish upon a prayer I can dream to touch anymore
The only thought of a memory, the only existence of love for me
To the thought of love that dwells within, no reason to pretend, while when I am with you, I can only feel gratitude for the flames within

...
I have loved, I have cared, in honesty and to cherish a love so fond, a bond that unites all of love that exist between us all
The only form of love that allows us to grow
The only existence to help us grow fond of all that darkness dwells to cover and to shade
A halo in camouflage, a feeling in distress, a feeling in such a disguise
I can only pray to wish upon a love once dreamt upon

...
When once I find myself within you, I would never ever leave
A dream I still dream
A star I still wish to grasp, the only star that I can see, the only vision that haunts my fading dreams

...
A once existing love of such purity, only happiness it would truly bring
"A Love In Darkness A Love To Fill The Hole Inside of Me"

To dream within a face to stare, to laugh with eyes in a blink of a glare
To try to believe, to do so in the act of leave, when having part of you, will fill the hole in me
To lose myself in the emptiness you bring, while even getting half of you, feels like everything

...

I dream of our kiss, whether it exist, to carry on this burden of such a love to give
If only I could be, if only I was, if only you were here, I wouldn't have to lose myself in the whispers lurking in the midst of the dark
Within an attempt to reach out to you, a golden flare of trust in bond, to cherish our last moment, I would give anything to be next to you again

...

In a wish of a prayer, I blink into a glimpse of a once existing feeling rushing to the boil point
Where love carries the torch that lights up the darkness in which I caress in the waves of her beauty
Such a view where I can only see, nothing except the beauty you glow
While drowning in the emptiness you bring, I follow the shadows into the abyss of forgotten memories
To dwell upon your lower back, to the touch of your shoulder as you always seem to move away
Always your laugh as we are kissing, trying to believe that this could be real
Instead of the feel of being trapped in my own haze of a lost reality

...

Believing that having part of you, will fill the hole in me
Cherish that only second to every minute I had trust in us
To forget what carried me so far and to lose sight of reality

Nothing comes close to touching the mark you have left inside of me
A love to cherish, a love to adore, a love to remember and to forever hold
Something so real, something so close
A love that exist and is accidental access in the feel of something so infinitely interesting

"A Strike Of Reflection In The Flicker Of My Dreaming Hand"
A flame begins to rise, a flame that ignites in the sparking reflection you bring in the glimpse of a fading memory
The close of a door, to leave every fear behind, only to wish to give you what you are giving me

...

You are the only thing, the only wish that makes me want to live at all

...

For when I am in sight of you, there is no reason to wish or to pretend, never a fault in a forward step
Only a chance of a halt, trapped in the spark that you ignite to a flame in the distance of another time and space of a shore to another land

...

Waves crash ashore and fade the memory deep beneath the ink where you have laid for a thousand years or more
Such a tragedy, the only woman I have ever truly adored
To speak upon, to dream of a star to bring you back to life, a touch so real, a touch to remember, a touch as such one can only hope to endure

...

Sharing this feeling I can only hope will reach into the conscious of thought
Where only the vision of you, a woman who once existed, the once only reason to where I prayed to exist within at all
A feeling of rush, to feeling of such craze, a wondrous sight of beauty so far beyond the reality of view
One can only dream to see, can only dream to hold
A love so pure, a love so honest and a love we all wish to share

While only a select few may ever have the chance to experience in a
hope of a prayer down a wishing well
A flame to feel, a flame that arose in the pit of darkness that was lit
by your stunning reflection in the flicker of this match that strikes in
a motion of my dreaming hand

"An Acquired Taste With Only Three Words Left To Say"
When well is not enough for me to dwell upon the wish for
something infinitely beautiful
In search of one to love, to care for and give my all
Only to find exactly what I have been wishing for, only to fall before
a guard wall
Once again another road block
So tear at these words and crush the feel, crush another grape in
order to flavor the wine
Such an acquired taste, just to find another way, another place to
settle alone and in peace
...
Well, well, well
I take it as that's love in its finest fashion, ring the bell before early
dawn
Just to be let down once more, so now I see the truth behind
A
"Cellar Door"
...
Within the wickedness of love, my hatred comes forth inside, to step
upon every emotion I think of accidental access
If accident means well instead of harm, would it change your mind
enough to give the opportunity
Instead I'm left with the slam of a door right before my eyes
A velvet sky before bloodshot eyes, when words speak the only truth
Nifty in the forthcoming of another phase to adore
And
I'm left with only three words left to say
...
Well, well, well

...

With a slam of the door right before my eyes, love must not exist, as tears fall again and I drop to my knees
I can only repeat the same three words
Well, well, well

"What You Think What You Seek Holds The Answer To What You
Will Find"
If I would have known in the darkened corner, that this would be the
only time I would see your face
With just one touch to your lower back, I place my hand just to
escape
In another way to describe a complicated way to accept
When everything that is new is nothing more than a lie

...

When all that I do brings me close to you, I begin to accept and take
back what was given to me
Find a way back to home in a place where the world goes away,
to breathe between the lines and conquer more than thought was
possible
When all that I see is a part of me, I will meet you where the river
takes me

...

The same sun within the same sky
God bless you son, at least you tried, but next time do instead of try
And
You will find comfort in the weakest moments of the present and
find the answers to what the future holds
Before the love that existed and to the future of love that is
nonexistent

...

Now I slow down, turn up the vibe over you
Within words that can't explain the beauty I see in you, when it's the
moment that won't let you down
With tears falling down, I seek and I find
A love to forever hold, to know that it is always around

When who am I to stay in this world that I made, just to watch as
you leave to move away, when how could I ever explain such a thing
The concept is eager, to the open of eyes, the taste of tears that
remind of what you feel and what you find
When the moment is what never lets you down
I hope and pray that it's always around for in the capture of love
I know that it is always around
What you think, what you seek, holds the answer to what you will
find
With one last reply I ask and I beg
Please don't lose something so beautiful, it is very lovely, when it is
what keeps me moving along
The moment you open your eyes, when we all think we are alive
Only the taste of tears is what reminds, that it is the moment that
won't let you down

...

What you think, what you seek, holds the answer to what you will
find
When it is only the moment that never cease to let you down

"Restless Within The Cute Boring Love I Endure Only To Wish Away"
With an embracing bad breath with smoke in eyes, covered in restlessness we cry
Love is too shy, to rise before the fate of demise, well, when every little second just flies as I stare into eyes as stunning as the stars in the sky

...

Break through the ride within the sunset, to ignore the cute of dignity inside the pride that crawls back into the emptiness of your heart
Praying just to live once more, loosing everyone I have ever loved
To share what signifies within a star lit bright, I want to fall in love and leave tonight

...

Only to ponder in such wonder, will I make it home alright, guide me as I praise upon a gentle stream of lies

...

Break through, what a thought, reaching deeply into what we find hard to comprehend, such as words described so beautifully
When love defines me, when every word seems so right
I only wish to fall in love and leave tonight

...

To switch the top of the line, with squealing of every cough within each breath that drifts astray
When I will never sleep alone nor love again
As they flock to me like an isle of open sores, a taste of such to die for
Lips to kiss, feel to touch, break the ignorance of speech, when I hide behind the love I once knew
Freeze without an answer and free from all of the shame

To live and breathe as one only to respond
"I will never sleep alone nor trust in love no more."

"In The Absence Of Love I Am A Mountain To Praise Upon Its People Below"
I have trusted in chapters that are bound to admit in defeat
I have captured trust in thee, back to home where I was waiting for love as a mountain, a gallop of hope in search of light of absence in the fall
To conquer sin, to trust in another, that's what this is all about
As flowers grew in the cracks of the ground that you paved, to imagine such warn that haunted my dreams
To groom my soul in harmony and peace, within a wish down a penny well
I cannot gather love anymore
...
Show me more than what is to be seen, ignorance is the statue that leans us downward into our greatest fall
I found the reason to leave you with this loan
When all I can do is to forgive your broken heart, trapped in this town that forms ambers in the burn
A torch like feel, in the grieve of absence, a love that exist no more
...
To gather my words and place upon the throne, such a heart to own is mine to care and yours to hold
Never the less to speak upon the riddle to belief that love is pure and possible
Show me the answer and I can trust in the wind while she paves me a different road
Then to start over only to choose something else
Pulled from the pages where the letters lack the pigment of trust
On my way back to where I feel forgiven and free from the broken love that has formed

...

I now stand as a mountain, a praise in the others, and the relapse to the fall

Searching for the lighthouse in the fog, maybe defeat is ok when it comes to love

To accept that opinion is only to be opinion based

With thorns in my waking dreams, I will never forget the constellation of our love

With hope and faith to mend the heart, I will rise up, beat every odd, just to show I am the light shining above

...

Gather your love, make it true, and find the reason to carry on your love

When all I can do is to forgive your broken heart

Trapped within the ambers of the deeply burned, I forgive myself and I have moved on

And

I believe you should do the same, maybe we will meet again, another time, another place, and another life maybe our love will forever hold true

Until then carry on in belief that love exist and the heart holds the key

Within every wish is a dream and every life has a destiny that you can redirect and conquer each star you wish to grasp upon

...

To be back someday would be beautiful, a subtle and soothing thought to endure

Never to abandon the outcome in search of the answer I deserve

While the chapters hold answers that prove the heart to be true

I will be back once more as a mountain to move searching for the lighthouse lost in the fog

Phase Three
"Covered In What Has Made Me The Path To Walk To Righteousness"

…

Covered in love to fill the gaps in disbelief by the ones who doubt the proof and if it is not as clear as you wish, then clarify for yourself by the truth of who you are
This is the fact that the believers are the fulfilled, with the act of faith there is no end to the dreams that you can reach upon

…

Within the heart is purity and control over one's mind set, why be at war with yourself
When it is easier to accept that there is a higher being looking over, but if you fail to believe in just something higher and failing to look up and pray for your own success and fulfillment
You may never be who wish to be especially if you fail to be positive and bring positive thoughts into your life and give off the energy into the atmosphere sending shock waves that shock in awe
Catching the air to breathe feels under the weather, under the basis if you walk the city streets only to ponder on why you feel so low of late
Show yourself the proof needed, the encouragement to walk and stand your ground
The strength to accept your wrongs
And
As always to continue upon your path to reach righteousness

…

This isn't about religion, this is clearly just to turn nonbelievers into believers of something higher than where we stand

For as we pray that at least our feet won't fail us and if we fall to have the will to stand back up and face our inner fears, within our future the goal is to never hold fear

When the secret is to believe in something and bring positivity into our daily lives

And

To pray that our feet will never fail again and forgive ourselves of our own sins

And

To correct our faults and turn them into new rights and face what we have feared for so long

"In Such Absurd Fashion I Gather My Praise Down The Flow Of A
Gathering River"
If god is love and love is real, bathe me in the cleanse of rejoice and
forgive my mistake, to my sinful charms, as a necklace I wore from
birth
Upon a smile that is fake upon my sorry face, within the capture of
love to the look of her dress
"Good God"

...

With fire in my ears, as the silence cowers over the halo of my lack of
sleep
When I don't need these voices ringing as church yard bells in my
ears
Repeating the same silence I have spoken all too well
Within the gathering of praise in attempt to reach the righteousness
I am in seek of, to hold as sand only to swing at some invisible hand

...

Correct my wrongs and hold the purity of faith as love in the beauty
that is all around to the true beauty beyond what the eye can see and
impossible to imagine such imagination of beauty to exist
More beauty than I can take, more beauty than I can even stand

...

If you are looking for a blanket my sweetheart, I am sorry I am no
such fabric
While you mumble your pitiful prayers in your tangled knotted sleep
As it flows in one river like the sharp down a mirror
Only to see yourself whole
And
You caress in its shiver

...

If the river is where I must pray then join me along my way, for this mountain we can move as the coldness is bitter and the movement we seek is only to continue forward

...

Charge at the waves, believe in the faith that can set this ship to safe sail, when the clouds bring such darkness as the hard rain begins to drown out fears we hang upon
While dreams lose their charm and I kept every old key just in case
Opened arms in case you need arms to wrap yourself around
The comfort of another is the belief of the start of something beautiful
In the end I won't let you go
Until the day I realized you were never mine at all to hold
As my exit was unfair and so absurd

...

"Lord have mercy and forgive me."

"Under The Willow I Embrace The Danger And Climb Each Mountain"
Lord I am here, standing next to the tower of dreamers, through this tale that represents the number ten
Cool as the wind blowing through the air under the willow tree, as tears fall, the sun and the moon shining galore, as the diamonds fill my heart and the outside of my skin glistening like the sun rays that give us the vitamin that equals happiness, fresh and feeling positive, there is no better feeling then waking up to the path to walk of the righteous ways of our leaders will

...

Back to the beginning when in this story of fear and all the way to love, when all I wanted was to run away yet, under the umbrella I whether the storm and within the attempt to reach out to the negativity to bring positivity in to all lives that cling to the willow I was trapped under
Weeping as the howl of the lone wolf, the flicker of the flame in the darkness, proves there is more beauty that is beyond conscious thought

...

Now continue to think upon the words written within ink wells and the feather pen to the pen creating the history we bled and fought for
Live and breathe and protect at all cost even as for our lives
For the children we will act upon the actions of doubt and anger of our enemies and give only truth behind hope to carry what is ours to hold and only ours to know

...

We share and they can't accept the reality of such beauty

Righteousness within each next step, the one above must be looking over the shoulder of the man with the feathered pen, spoken as one such as another creating history
Wisdom and courage to stand up for what is in belief, what can be known as knowledge?

...

Take a breather and rest your tired eyes, get back up and repeat the last words to remember what is beyond the metaphors, within the timing and the lines, letters are written about phases we all face as face to face actually means nothing, when every mountain needs to be conquered, justify the fact of the earning and continue on

...

The righteous ways are not far ahead, with true belief in acceptance of who you are and love for yourself
You will succeed and rise over every next mountain until you conquered every struggle and happiness is yours to forever to claim

...

Happiness is the secret key, face the danger you encounter with faith in yourself
"You Will Not Fail

"Questions Repeated Only To Be Asked And Answered By Such Liars"
To dream of the path that I walk to lead me to righteousness, while only a few leagues off the shore as the taste of the kiss, the last I was to know
With a blank smile upon confessions set so long ago
As
We keep our prayers so short

...

Sink the sail, sink the ship set free to sail, why this distance with a curious look within the pluck of a single string
If you are afraid then I am afraid, knowing we do not have to be afraid anymore

...

Drown in the cleansing, dance to the preaching of another sad song and caress in my notion to the sound waves of deep breathing to relax such intense hyperventilation
While I was to become the servant of all, with the cup in my hand for all to sip upon
Such a taste one to die for, one to forever cherish yet, only once we may adore
Forever to hold

...

Within my attempt to see, in such miserable time, I heard there was a cure for human sight

...

Crash waves, crashing ashore the righteousness I was to adore, as leaves wilted as petals fall hopelessly to the soil
Am I who I am or do I need more grace than I thought

Will someone answer me, within a hot cloth over my forehead, time is getting fast as I grow old quicker than before

...

Such subtlety and if I ask the same question, when I know I ask the same questions, it's because everyone who answers me I know is a liar

...

Righteousness is beauty, mine to cherish for all to see, for all to share, the concept of life the secret to your questions, the answers are near

"Righteousness Found Within The Seek To Find What We Thought Was Not Possible"
Within each attempt of resilience, the stars remain, feel the flames deep within the sigh of relief, such a beautiful feel of pain as yesterday's tears fade in the abyss, the smoke rises in the frame, a phoenix burn in the catch of righteousness

...

Glory may be in each who seek such beauty to feel and beauty to see

...

A dig between the burial site, to forever tarnish the existence of evil, what if the so called stance of what is the vision portrayed is the answer we all are in seek of
With honor in our move to the right not to the wrong of the mistake, cherish this life and seek the righteousness ways, not the wicked, only the miracle of such grace of beautiful pain in feel

...

Within each attempt we dig inside to carry the treasure of what is exactly the purpose behind the quarter down the penny well, for the righteous ways in our decisions of our own wicked ways

...

With damage to our hearts, within each medication to strengthen another part of us that is out of control, another sign of righteous ways to have what is needed to gain the courage to stand for ourselves and crush the demons that enter the forbidden thought cycle
We stand through it all and live to breathe and stand tall, for in the end when righteousness we seek
And
Righteousness is ours to hold and forever to cherish
Happiness takes over our thoughts, such a beautiful way to feel, a learning curve to strengthen ourselves that we never sought or

thought could exist, when so much beauty surrounds what we
cannot see, until we seek righteousness and righteous we may be
And
Righteousness is ours to be and to forever to adore
A world we can only dream of, until that world becomes our own
Reality

Phase Four
"The Extinguish Of Love The Hurtful Words The Curse To Set Me
Free"

…

The curse has her bed written, I heave at the drain in a rhythm to the
war drums
Such beauty before my eyes that I can never overcome, to stay in
silence the only language that I can speak within the scenes vision set
to overcome

…

Travesty led me to stray where I can no longer view the beauty that
was once before my eyes, while dizzy and clearly unable to just let this
go

…

While I surrender to the remedy of the unknown
Catch me and heal me, lift me back up to the sun where I choose to
live

…

Only exception takes away the promise, the gift and the curse that
shy's away the phantom of positivity

…

Such beauty to catch me and heal what is the cumber of my reflection
While I choose to live

…

Only when I realize she is no longer mine
Dreaming to be lifted back up to the sun
Where I ask to survive the bottom

…

Only dreaming to choose to live, counting hands before the rosary
beads

Driving another nail before another needy hole

...

Please believe in my own regret to ask before the throne of age that I will be set free from this curse and shallow waters will hold no ground over my own gift

...

Where I will no longer surrender to the remedy of the unknown
The only place where I can be healed

...

Where I will certainly choose to live
"The Unsighted To The Great Curse So Uninvited"
Can I win just one time, for within the survival of this condition when your cut I will bleed
Slowly severing the only memories that bind us as one
When I only know how to lose with you, when to win would be a dream come true

...

I'm starting to feel a transformation, how did I get here? Only to not recognize my own reflection, just a ghost of what once was

...

Within the shame of the beauty, I seem to collapse in its place and face the scar to be left behind
To realize my own truth, did I really speak those words, the Cinderella that I disgusted, what a phrase, in my attempt of my own guilt and shame

...

So pitiful that I was, should have seen this, my attempts, my own words all along
Built upon burial, just as beautiful as you are
Only your beauty can lift this curse

Such beauty that should have allowed me to see this coming all along
...
So mister unknown, what is your excuse, face the truth and the answer is loud and clear
When there is nothing more to lose, what is simply your excuse?
...
Within this phase I have seen my attempts in built foundation
Collapsing between the age of whispers, floating gently across the praying stream
Only in time to be set free, lifted of the curse I set myself
To dream in motion picture, I view myself as one deeply disturbed within the scar that she left behind
Such beauty never to see nor never, to be found or hear of again, no not anymore

...

A hero in language, the founder of a pure loving heart, left to rot between his own cursed life and the reality he can never grasp. Knowing and loving all, only to repeat the forbidden phase over and over, he crosses the trials and error after error, he forgets how to love and forgets how to make two as one. Losing grasp on himself and falling into the bed of sorrow surrounded by roses he lays in a sorrowful bed, awaiting for his curse to be set free, for the love of his life to lead the search they wander and ponder for years to come. Dreaming of something with so much more than this, only to still find the beauty that rest deep within the foundation of this curse. A foundation built upon envy made just for him by the unknown of this world, to keep the purity away from understanding, trading his soul for misunderstood explanations, with the look towards the sky they just could never fully understand what it was all meant for.

"Covered In The Curse To See And Realize Once More"
A curse that led me to stray down within a hole, grasping onto what is left to hold, to treasure the extinguish of the curse that follows, illness that covers this disease, transforming me into what I must not believe

...

Follow my prints for the love you seek must be to admit, free from the guilt you chase after
Once in my own blank mind the treasure speaks, curse to lift, curse to live, follow my prints to capture the rapture

...

The pearly gates open wide to set me straight, follow what the travesty leads to be the freeman across the white halls as we dance in laughter
Only the fall from grace can escape my embrace, when orders seem wrong and in doubt I must choose my own destiny, to find the right in choice, the opposition of my own face
To the beauty I see god has set to replace, while in my stay I pray and fight for him to see there is still beauty left for himself

...

This fight I must lead myself, I will no longer stand my ground, I will fight for all who seek the right in choice
"God we just want to stay home."

...

Within every simple choice lays the wrong decision, we must notice before it is too late and the path to righteousness closes in on our own sin and the curse is to be lifted among our burial ground

...

"You can fight!" God screams aloud. I find within my broken soul, God has left his throne

While in my journey I find the mischief upon his belief, I will no longer stand for this uncommon statue of common disbelief

...

"Lord, you have given birth to us, you cannot just give up and you have preached this to us for far too long for you to be in disbelief of your own creation."
I have breathed in the fresh air of birth and have tasted the face of death
Only beauty covers this curse far too stretched, cover me and I will cover you
Detach and I will reattach skin to bone and heart to soul
If you fail to believe I will make you see the light of realization that belief created a new open door only for you to see beauty once more
"Beauty In Hurtful Words That Was Within The Hand I Was Dealt"
I spoke those words so hurtful, cover the tracks that remember the past
If I could take them back, I remember, oh girl I forget everything that I have said, when I only wish to make you feel special, beautiful the last on the list to speak such hurtful words that I wish I could take back, never meant a word, for this curse has the best of what dwells deep within this heart of mine

...

When words crush the grape to flavor the wine, I wish to slow down the visions that relapse every memory that tears me apart
When the basement is full of anger for myself, such words to speak aloud
Shallow budget, to every word I extinguish, a fire arose within the deepest of secrets
When I relax every word comes out exact, one more then I'm done, did I ever really matter to you

...

I'm not saying that I won't break another heart, when the breaking is not purposely dealt
Only the cards fall into place and I play the hand

...

When feelings come and I hide them so well, bury my corpse and let the pieces lie just where they fell
When the open car is the last smell, after the draw of line is the truth of the proof to everything

...

Wish in doubt and toss a penny down the well, cover your prints as the devil passes to follow, hair blowing in the wind of an open car

...

Beauty was the last smell for me, only beauty that I could see
When beauty is there for me to read
Your face is all that I can see
Such words I wish I could replace
Such time for me to wish I could replace with charm in action to make you feel special
With this curse none of this actually seems possible, a shame in guilt, a shame in the cards that I have been dealt

"A Close Of Door To Close Of Eyes Barely Optimistic To Travesty"
Close my eyes just to look at you, taking by the scenes vision, ignoring illness, turning blue what a lovely color, taking up by my own demise for you

...

Clashing waves to the shore of my own lost reality, while I never wanted to know
Closer to the approval, while I just ignore the smoke and smile, while I lay beyond the bed in view and such a perfect color for your eyes

...

When in search to doubt, I close the blinds to sit and stare at you

...

Laying gently by your side, I take your hand and follow my own mind. While I never wanted to know. Closer than I ever was, proud and in my own shame to allow you so close. Bed written in a travesty, now you're here and I'm so far, only to feel your hand in mine. Only for once more, before your eyes close and you drift where I can no longer see.
While strangers pass and I can't care, to vanish today and close the door to the last opening of my own will

...

What am I to do with all of this silence, a gift and a curse, side by side, within my attempt to heave at the drain for silence is to cover the cumber of my own reflection
While moving away is only to say I am better off without you and to forget the past and what I have said, side by side, only to feel your hand grow so cold and your eyes shut

...

To realize you were never here at all

"The Health Of Another Is What I Live And Die For"
As dead as dead can be, such hurtful wine flavored travesties, cover the blanket, for star holes have lately been the wires and the fuse to blow me away

...

Leaning over you here, cold and catatonic, to dream in visions of the color blue within the means to become my own perfect enemy
To dream in better ways, to forgive what I have said, a wish in doubt, a dream into cast
When I am better off this way, wake up and face me, while someday I will walk away only to say you have disappointed me, oh Lord, you have finally disappointed me, sick of all of this false relationship contrast fading into the darkness of where I can never repeat those most sacred words

...

Where are the angels and the stampede for I feel like swimming in the drowning of the abyss
Lost and foreseen sights such as the perfect death of me

...

So wake up and see beyond what the eye can see, when travesty can be beautiful in every way
A brief reflection of this curse, so burn all that's left of me

...

Cold and in harm
Travesty at its best
Wide and in the open
Why can't you turn and face me
When all you have done is disappoint me
So sick of all of this, I turn to lift the curse and be set free
And

Fall back in love with my own created destiny

...

I can't ask you for much more, when the health of the others is what I live and die for

...

To smother the corresponding act and cover the tracks of its debris, where only we have been the joke of the tune, in only the interest when there is nothing else to do. This curse is made to be my bed of flowers to surround my cold body upon living and in death, for one day to be set free by such a love who has read and was born to be. Only to caress in her arms am I to speak one last time the most sacred words
"I Love You..."
As I believe in silence can raise this curse that has been placed upon my soul beyond what can be understood in every way. Distance can measure the length but nothing can measure the amount of love I have for the one who will lift this curse and finally let me be set free. Fresh air, breathing in the silence and the motion of this world's nature, such beauty I then repeat, over and over until it is time for me to finally
"Rest In Peace...I Still Love You...Words Are Fueled Devices"

Phase Five

"The Story It Told Held The Belief In Everything Will Be Alright"

...

We walk these paths and travel our roads, distant in thoughts that never seem to end in roam. We wish upon stars that never see our light yet, only feel our energy. We bring the pain to the rest. We capture then release as our hearts seem dead inside. To remain dead inside we must sacrifice our pain for faith and find our way. Never be discouraged for in thee we can be practical and extraordinary. Each of us can pray along the praying stream. When every single day and in every single way, we drag ourselves down, when all we need is to believe and learn to appreciate what is real and forgive ourselves and let go of the pain we feel and realize what is real.

...

Within a blink and a tear for another's suffering we can gather praise in a way never seen before and call out our steps and join the others along our path and begin our own adventure to love and righteousness. Calling on behalf of those who care and those whom love and see our future as the brightest star to have ever shined above and die in life's never ending cycle.

...

To say we have seen enough is never enough to examine. When we believe all damage is done, that is just the start of another rebirth. We can hang onto ourselves with a lend of a hand of another. A willing heart to sacrifice. When we believe in something, we make belief in something greater than sin and trust is built and love is shared, so these stories may fill your heart with sorrow only through metaphors speak of such tales that fill you with joy and purpose to continue in the darkness of shadows with whispers that lurk in corners awaiting our bliss. To find the strength we begin to melt into what we call a metaphorical change, a process of cell restructure to find our own true selves. Keep your head up and believe in a change for the better and believe that these words will heal. When the waves crash ashore words of the tales you seek will heal the deepest of wounds and change our hearts and guide thee on the loft quest with the motivation to never speak out upon fake prodigy, only trueness in pure love and pure belief.

...

"The Incident"

He knelt down before her grave with wishes upon praying wells. A taunt haunts him within a cool shiver from across the whispering breeze that passes as a slight reflection of what once was only a dream. His eyes begin to dwell on the past as if there is something left to prove. A fever begins to drown his sorrows and tomorrow he sees sunshine. Within lack of control he falls before the grave of the ones he loves, the one he loved more than himself. Tears fill like puddles of beading drops of rain in a silhouette. Followed by the leave and the grief, he draws the line, he screams out loud, "I'm taking control and I am shutting you out with no doubt this is my time to shine, before all who knelt down once before." In a cast of rage, like animal fever a sense of calmness caresses his soul, for in this moment he proves to himself that the unfortunate accident of six will not forever haunt his mind, yet fuel his motives for his life. The future still holds true to his thoughts to prove. The climb out of the dwellers cell, he traps the beads of sweat between his eyes and draws a line upon the floor and once he crosses this line he is shutting that fatal accident out.

Several months have passed and he has stayed true to his thought to prove. His wishes, the energy he sent into the universe has surrounded him with the passion to never move from positivity, like a twist of fates rules, like a twist in plot that patches a hole of abuse. He has begun new and exciting activities such as a daily journal, daily workouts and proper eating habits to sustain a healthy mood. He can't deny himself a snack to crave every once and while, only to find when he indulges in squander of self-abuse to only remember what he has proved to forget. Suddenly the day was brought back when he lost all control and the thoughts raged passed one after one, like a sudden shout from a mountaineer. His inner core racing with internal fear of what is to come or that has already been undone. The accident that led him to stray was exactly as he had planned a loss of control at the steering wheel. A loss of focus led the car astray from the path and verging into an oncoming lane. No one reacted to such attention that was staring them right in the eye, such as facing a great white along the shore line. A compassionate kiss that led to the abuse to this twist of rules and the hole it leaves. The car was in a loss of control and as he kissed and tasted her sweet innocence for the last time he faced forward into an unnoticed collision about to explode. At fifty seven miles per hour he drove a car of five passengers including his wife and four kids straight into the line on the bend of a hill head on into a semi and at that moment, right before impact he knew right there and then his life was to forever change, but there was no hope for the gain of control. The car hit the semi and flew to the left over the rail and down a seventy foot drop and there it laid before his eyes, his family at rest and also the driver of the semi who managed to stay on the road, only in the end to cause more ill to his own sake and peace of mind. This incident he now begins to realize five years to this date will never vanish nor disappear it is to forever stay, just as the words forever my dear. His heart once again broke into two, a man set on auto tune or cruise control a lack of conscious and improved self-abuse. He has now lost all control as he grips the frame of all that he had once before, a wife to adore and his children to miss only more and more. He grabs the bottle and begins to drown as if it was a grown passion just to self-induce a sleep or two that only led to a worsened mood. When finally the shutting out and all of the progress that lay out before was about to hit rock bottom. He starting clawing his way through curtains and throwing fist after fist into hollow woodened walls, trashing everything he came across, in a blurry state of vision, making his way into the closet where the mystery solves the puzzle. A gun therein lies upon the floor, hidden behind a loosened hitched cornered door. He grabs the gun and kneels before his reflected image in the standing mirror calling out, " Is this what you want from me Lord, another death upon my bloody hands, another soul for the Devil to claim, my own life the only thing left for me to abuse. Fine then." He grasps the gun as tight as he could shaking to the irrational thought that was laid between his eyes like sweat again as beads between his mind blurring every thought into a negative thought and a mountain to climb. "Enough Lord" He screams, the owls begin to howl and the crows begin to call and just as the church yard bells ring for the last time in his own mind, he pulls the trigger with a bite of the tongue and now there are seven laid out before, an unfortunate accident that could have been avoided, yet he craved her kiss so much he risked everything and in the end it cost him seven total lives including his own, seven bodies now buried down near the moor. Written upon the gravestone, "A Loving Father and Husband, one to adore and to forever remember, Rest in Peace within the Heavenly skies." Those were the words that we all will remember, not this unfortunate turn of events but the heroics of a life that stood before, a waiting in progress, just another tale of life to truly adore. To realize that life is to forever cherish because of the simple fact that we all seem to forget, that life can be taken from us at any moment, during anytime. For these words are to hold onto and keep in mind, to love the ones you love and always show it, live your life to the fullest and never give up on anything, follow your dreams every second that this world twirls. We learn that people come and go only in physical form but as for souls they forever live on, so trust and believe, keep faith at an all-time high and your soul will be set free to live on in peace and harmony

"The Bird That Could Never Sing Before The Gallows...Never More"
For love we may, to wish and exist, to carry our burden, to treasure our chest. Within its warmth of comfort of our souls. A desire such as to see, as one is to feel. A captain set to sleep before the wheel and a crow to dance along the shore, a worm within the hole and a sheep to gather my coat, floss before my teeth, between the outskirts of land as I only pretend to be the man I wish I can.

...

The raven flew above the night with stars dreading the scare less flight, a sink beneath my bones wither before the prey of my own guilt, you may wish, you may prance in glory before the guidance of righteousness only to adore what you have never knew of before.

...

The man took the flock of raven dust and blew the final corpse into the air. Before too long the raven crept into see, what could have been or what he could see. The bite and thrust to the ravens touch an evil so great only the lord above of lightening must be struck. To take the stroll into the pluck of each eye, the man was given no sight to what could be ahead to enlighten or to adore. A dream of the raven to wish to just exist, may we quote the never more or to simply pray before the ravens dust and dream of the day the curse was lifted and the old man was in dwell for the pluck of each eye from the raven who sang never more.

"The Sacred Souls In Seek To Gather His Praise In Peace And Harmony"
Broken bells ringing in and out of deaf ears as they bled for the healing of the North Star, wicked in harm and transformed once righteousness has been adored. With hope in our prayers, our holiness shall forgive or forsake within attempt to never be bleak, only to rest within thee that counters the fault of each movement.

Look how soon we all fail and assume, when only so soon we will improve. Take each thy words and gather where he lay, under the sun and the moon as one and take thy flight and grasp its wisdom and knowledge and be led to expand his kingdom.

...

We gather around the flowing energy, to sanctify in his certainty of existence, we look up and howl up at whom may be staring back at our fiber glass ghost eyes, with bearing points of thoughts we only thought we were to know. Half hazard-less we hide and cumber underneath the cove while your hands are wrapped around mine as the explosion of the tiny prayer balloon broke our back.

...

Slept until I had no more, mercy was felt then ignored, showering into the midst of what is to adore as a push from the rise, she shook her head and I said "No either do I."
Sailing past the archer song when our thoughts simply never meant a thing when he only asks that we do as we praise the honesty in trust in thee as he may wish upon and us just to sever the tides and do our part.

...

You can cry in forgiveness asking louder than his reply, searching for your next travesty, with my selective memory in phase unknown as the no named author aimed this at the ones who are uncertain of this. Looped and tightened while no one can be the one who can, unless you wrap yourself around the songs of rejoice and feel his presence in which we seek to sought and to believe only set to one day retrieve.

...

A memory exist within our hearts deep within, buried under his love, where he carved his name to remind us he is there and has sent out his words and answers as his silent reply.

...

Hallelujah

"Strengthen Your Weakness As I Am Your Sacrifice"
I traveled this road many times before, trampling over each step as if each one was backwards. A lending hand to help me back upon my feet. Within such grace he speaks to me. His words with such beauty of each wakening tale of harmony.

...

I am now in seek of medical mercy within the tragedy of self-abuse, when my little girl so beautiful, with air so thick I can hardly breathe. When I reach out for his hand, tell me now, ask me now, when it is difficult to stand up straight. An answer in a shame to lose a little girl so beautiful, I am petrified of losing my life to breath. I could never gather in praise to you. I only seek what is truly beautiful, within separate homes we must conquer this debate. Over and out, I cry to the heavens for the strength to carry this burden, the weight upon my shoulders.

...

I feel the strength begin to weaken my knees, such a formula to be so meaningful, righteous in my own way. A strength picks me up, no more fog, it is easier to breathe within the strength of the wounded is where I can be found, just as Christ I am to preach of courage through these lessons I have learned. Battle to begin the dispute of no more violence when we believe we must act upon vengeance to cure our own past wounds, when no one can answer the corrections, I stand as the fault to take the blame so you can cherish life in itself and strengthen your weakness, my blood is your thirst, hammer the nails and I will be your Holy Sacrifice.

"Smile Lines Between The Patience To Just Breathe"
When I wake up I tell myself to look at my face, feel so funny, within the blink of an eye. Capture the war cry, when it hurts, I cry and scream at the top of my lungs. Am I ok today?

...

Within the blink of terror, to terrorism of myself, a blink of faith, only to self-induce a sleep, just to not scream of the terror of my bloody nightmares. When I wake up I am afraid I might have pissed my bed, oh my Lord, just take these dreams away for I am in shame of the break, to all of the things that leave me faceless, breathless, and cornered in mischief of what is the cause to my own forsaken thoughts. Can you believe in my own praise, to dream out loud to you? Now to day two of the terror I fear yet, when pretty faces pass I am afraid to look up, a blank stare is what she receives, no smile, for thy lines have worn out, a blank shadow of his Holiness. Leave me in a trial of my belief and I will take each blow to the heart as I always have, so when I wake up I tell myself to look at my face and to not feel afraid for this is still my face and my own beliefs and there is no reason to be afraid of anything. Let us be patient and follow my own creativity, make a dream and leave your mark upon his grace.

...

Wake up for it is a brand new day to count your blessings and gain your courage to stand and fight our demons and move past our limits and never fear, for it is all in our heads of make belief. Dream and follow your path to be who you were destined to be, there is no need to be scared to breathe and no one should make you feel so afraid to stare at yourself.

...

When I feel ashamed, I splash cold water upon my bloody nightmares that count souls to sleep. Shaping the inner core for the war in terror of my inner being and react upon my own dream to self-detain what it is that makes me so scared. Faith in glory, faith in my belief will get me through all of this, no need to cry, no need to scream at the top of my lungs. When it is only the Lord and me anyway, so shape my core to fight for the strength to witness and adore the stars for they represent all that we are, our Mothers and Fathers, Gods eyes are the Sun and the Moon.

"Awaiting Love To Destroy Every Caress Of Your Touch"
In every waking moment of believing you wish I would say yes to your mission to set it in stone. Where can I hide, when every face is staring at the portrait that resembles me? Every trouble with keeping it inside these walls, what a subtle defeat to cease. When I find a hole to bury myself in just to close this statement of truth, when the truth is the false in the right to choose.

...

The more I have dreamed, the more I have forgotten and I have ended up alone with everybody watching me. With the tune in my ears, ringing alarms bringing the charm of self-defeat. When everybody is watching me wallow in my own self-defeat. Walking once more on my own, trample again over steps of stone, telling the truth is harder than speaking in tongues of lies, just as simple of a lifeless soul. I must carry out this order of control. Gather the stones, stone after stone, place them gently upon the praying stream, because when the more I am left alone, the more I am ok. When all I want is for everybody to stop watching me.

...

Hollow to the swallow of the plan of the year which I would end up to fear. Only love is the feel, the only words you could say, when she was just enough for me, to put your love in a bag and she said you better never leave me, only awaiting the downfall. Every time I try to love it begins to be so adoring and flawless just as the beauty you carry.

...

Ruffled and swayed, oh so loving and flawless, just waiting for the destruction of the both of us.

...

With everybody watching me, it seems the entire time they were also watching you.

...

So adoring and flawless, I can't stop to think more on the beauty that your touch caresses when I add it all up, the problem with love is I end up lost and become careless because of your flawless attributes, only awaiting the downfall of our loves destruction. When no more, no less, I will not wait on love, I will bury this hatchet and dispose of any remains that I was even here. Your love carried me this far and meanwhile I was awaiting this day for our love to be destroyed by my own hand, so don't cry my sweetheart. It will be alright, everything will be alright in the end.

"The Power We Search Is Not Within One Only Within Us"
It all began with the curiosity to the diamonds he wore upon the hands that could be the filth of a land under killing for the money under the rocks and stones in the streams.
There is no way this could be happening he believed in yet, when he sought out his beliefs, he began to believe in the filth and chose to believe in the right of the choice to stand up and use his voice to protect the word Amen.
When they say diamonds are the most precious pieces of the earth. We forget the violence that went on in Africa just to make money to bring children in while making them kill their own families, then to teach them to shoot an AK at the innocence. We in thee need more leaders, this is a message to all of those who can't believe this is all happening, when it's an everyday activity to make money off ignorance.
With belief in hope we can make this a forever change, when a voice is the leader of fear, love, righteousness and the curse to be set free

of our everyday life. Demons tracking every movement in attempt to slow us down. Even with the Gods looking down upon each of us, believers or not.

It simply doesn't matter when hope and pure belief is enough to make it through. When the diamonds shine in the sunlight we should be in the wonder of where it all began for the right in choice of which diamonds we carry on through the family tree.

Blessings can be sent over the filth of these diamonds and the lives killed over the priceless jewels this earth has granted us.

Pure voices can cure this world of harm, with imagination take this roller coaster and picture many lives living in innocence being slaughtered and tortured to work under the pressure of never knowing when their days are done.

Picture innocence crossing your path with a gun pointed at you demanding you to work for nothing while living in fear of knowing your family could be raped and killed any second and there is nothing you can do, when there is no sense in modern days.

People need to see the wrongs, the filth that cover the governments that could care less of the people that make this world what it is, for in the power of each of us and if you feel you have no power and or no gift, then it's time to find your inner self, search for what lies deep within your personal basement while crossing bridges only you can cross because it is only your path, the light will shine when the Gods call upon you to make your final move, the choice you make of your voice can make history or you will be forgotten.

In my experience your voice is the power that no one can cure only unpredictable. Speaking from your soul is the power you need to search for. When the message is right before your eyes but you refuse to see the light.

That is the sign you need to believe in a higher power and then he went to the leaders and prayed for the power to speak and his voice shed light upon the Heavens and he made history for speaking out upon his true beliefs, something he never thought to be possible, when the impossible is always possible when Faith enters your soul.

Miracles are everyday secret alarms and when you hear the bells ringing in and out of your ears you are one of the voices to preach out upon what we need to change ourselves to care.

With care and love for others, with hands together and praise to our Gods we can send our message to the whole world that would make the change needed to save ourselves and save the lives who are next to go, exactly what is needed to share our power not within one or within you, but within us.

"A Pull Upon The Tip Of Your Heart"
I am looking for its relation and I believe we were made right from the start. When your wings hovered over graces of love. I have stood in wonder, claiming to be a man. With wishful thinking I pray for you not to take your love from me, "Oh dear Lord just let her go!" I scream at the roof of two tongues. Placed into insightful vision, I can only pass to still ponder, if we were meant to be right from the start.

...

To clarify my reason, I must measure the instrument to desires, find my coursing levels and to find that you have now have none. Tears form into a liquid, racing through every thought, only to find myself lost and alone In a world I feel so small in and only one window for me to peek out from.

...

Love is the kind of thing you never get with just looking, it's the kind of thing you never think of and it is the level of our hearts and of what we were made of, desires and weakness.

"The Eyes Of A Little Girl That Led Me To Righteousness"
Wishing to be true, is to be not true. Doing to be true, is to be purely true. May you only need the light when the candle is burning low, let my love fill you with the joy and happiness to carry on. For I must say goodnight with tears in my eyes. You will always be my little girl, no matter how far or near you are at this moment.

...

Listen close and close your eyes, may whispers of the angels burn away the rapture your heart fears. The terror you have seen and felt, mother hit hard and threw across the floor by the evil in man. Listen baby girl, I may not be your father, but I am always here, for I love you so and I will never let you go. If I went into what hides behind the closet in the dark, it would be hard for you to sleep, so let me read frog and toad and watch you as you rest your eyes as the angels sing you to sleep.

...

As I watch you grow from afar, it tears at every single thread in my dying heart. I try to say hello, but it seems you always beat me to the punch, then a close of the door,
the most beautiful angel child disappears never knowing when I will see your face again. Only loving since I held you for the first time and I would never let you go.
A promise I knelt before to always keep.
That promise has led me this way to watch you grow to where you are today from afar I say I still love you so, my sweet baby girl.

...

We shed to wake up in mourn, we bleed so others can be free.
Let the tears roll down our cheeks, for in our hearts is where the real beauty is kept. In darkness we kneel before our gods and embrace the choice to decide. Never let fear take the wheel of your own life. Be

the reel off the hook, be the one who knows oneself true. Always fall asleep with a smile in the shape of gratitude. Give help when a hand is in reach and you will see how much is to be returned, only if you believe it so.

...

A joy and sensation we cannot control what takes over and burns away our hatred, leaving behind only the love that we have been missing for so long. While watching the sunrise upon the horizon of the road to righteousness, we are blessed to say I have shed tears to this.

...

Love is pure and true, only fake if it is in bad company, keep love close and you will be forgiven and peace is yours in reach.

Never let go of what you hold true to yourself and the highroad is finally yours after troubling paths and errors and if you love her, never let her go,

because you will only realize just how much when you let her go, so now you know.

...

"Dear angels that fight to keep me alive, one day I closed my eyes and then I understood why, my little girl that I must love afar, keep every word close to your heart and I promise the light will always shine bright upon your soul. Never dwell on what the past has brought or what the future may bring, just love what is now and the people you have had the chance to love and I promise I still hold my promise true that I still love you so."

...

Take charge of your life and learn to give more than receive, find yourself, your inner being and complete yourself and help complete this world and fulfill your own.

...

"Every Journey Begins With One Small Step, Keep Belief And The Blood We Spill Will Fill Our Hearts With What Is Real Instead Of The Pain We Once Believed Was Real."

Outro

"Life's Riddle In Pure Belief"

...

We must believe that within believing we could overcome any obstacle that we come across and become the person we have always dreamed to be. Through struggles and fear we lay down in mercy only to be left behind in each waking act of sin. With only sweet memories of what once was. After this read, we can learn to cherish those around us and those who seek happiness and righteousness through the wounds that bleed. Holding hands together we can become one in awe. In the shock of awe to the beauty that sways still before our eyes, we can behold the truth to ourselves. When every second is time we can follow every word like street lights and hold onto what our heart desires in life, just as love we can hold no fear for the rest of our lives and learn to truly breathe and to truly live.

Encore

"The Answer Lies Beneath The Ink"

...

Why so curious, to bring past to present, only to understand why it was forgotten in the first place? Was it a justification or Realization of your Heart left shattered by the guilt and of the shame in which cards were so called magically before me. What such Beauty rises beyond the mend of this blessed curse, to be set free is but a wish, while the dream is to be truly Living until the card is flipped and my time has come to pass onto Lighter and Brighter days, which stills upon a center Mantle, my source of oxygen to be deeply breathing, allowing a strike of the burst that allows each letter to piece back together in the phase of After Earth. A puzzle of such a Wondrous view to explore. Ignoring the warning signs, I go down the same old Road, over and over, just to help soothe and let the mind repeat the same throw down of a noose feeling to endure.

Puzzled...Troubled...Confused

Only to be the One and the Only, "So Called by too many to even count or keep even a slightly accurate single number." When I am lost with no stars in sight, to guide me through this maze, I stumble to pray, stuttered in acceptance to what Reality has brought straight before my feet, Brick after Brick.

Now my path has been granted to the concept of sight, laid out, leading upon a personal thrown for the only souls who have faced such travesties with such a height where no one else has ever reached to grasp, find, and to seek the furthest star and turn fantasy to dream, dream to focus, and focus into succeeding on the only thing left to Love."

To taste the grasp and shake upon your own successful living, proving the impossibility of an act most likely to be the life to have.

When told to be nothing more than just a Dream, such a shallow, stapled, and selfish phrase praised upon by so many, such weakness and missed through perspective, correctly detached.

Souls afloat, the oxygen based floor, still with mixed approaches to act upon when the time comes to climb or cowardly reject to be better, just as Life has no meaning, or is it fun to fail, suddenly, whiplash of the certainty that certainty does exist and if seen, it is possible for one to seek and for one to reach persuaded by the ringing churchyard bells, screaming of darkness and whispers of such a day to pass to be forever remembered.

The definition of all the exhausting, tiresome, and troubling choices wished away, only to reappear, to keep self-intact, from time to time self-check that at least you remember who you truly are, as to what is their appearance, only to focus on placing each misplaced piece together, to gather to Perfection.

A Portrait to the very important specific Word Placement, so Masterfully connected to you as this will always leave you Speechless and Breathless, sunk in the twisted craze seeping in the seeking of the spiral of overwhelmed emotions portrayed, to be left to feel the purest form of real feeling, whether it ends with the good or the bad, it is now what you have made it and led it to be. With the beginning of this mistake brought upon the most honest and heartfelt Work of Art creator, who remains ignored from interest, the panic button dual set to auto freeze time, out of Earth and Between All Afterlife's contracts, to truly think deeply into a Single Choice that you have to debate under, which the certainty of your existence takes its role and as your own choice, you create who you become. How hard to Believe it is that easy, when you take no personal interest to take the time to step into a true belief of your own, then to realize what is really missing. To the facts, you have blinded yourself from the Most

Glorious view to the eye, for within the Word and Thought of belief lies the truth of Imagination and how to view what you have kept Hidden away for so long. Now it has imploded into thoughtless and careless acts that affect the course of your future positioning, so to react in the correct manner is not your first choice on how to choose, which then places you in denial and self-harming reactions to major and also minor fears that attack like the viewing of a ghost peeking through the lonesome window, a view so familiar to them, that you look like you're in the transformation process to rot away within the Abyss, but with just enough strength from the one reaching to catch you falling. You awake and realize the mainframe, the main source to Life's Lost Riddles was a vision sought to attention as an urgent message, where trapped within is your key and placement of the door, so stop the wandering and let the path lead you to float in Happiness. When put to the test I came out the best climber and left so much to ponder forever, that may never be answered, but do not take every word as Truth for it may also be a disguise for they are each one or the other, but either way you can find the meaning, for what was claimed to be fictional, held more truth than is understandable and even comprehendible, so who could it be, but myself, if all of those words and tales came from my never ending speed train thought cycle in mostly thoughts and emotions, that create the chills that send the awaiting shiver, for those who choose to see into you as you and word for word, in the attempt to not look at me as me, but my words and feelings as happy yet, unsteady past life choices to live reckless, for their true reason and meaning that was placed and intended to have to be Reached for and Found as pieces of Life's Lost Riddles, comprehendible to only be effective sense of taking apart and putting back together in order and follow the steps or stated as rules for self-acceptance and True Happiness.

...

"The Answer...Beneath The Ink."
The Answer To Happiness All Along Was Hidden By The One, who carried it so deeply buried. The Crown of all treasures, The Pursuit of Happiness within the palm, or so they all say. "Statement or question, please state purpose for previous statement made?" "Well, if they all Truly Believe, then so must I..."

...

Accept and move forward, we are all capable and worthy to owe thyself at least that much.

...

"To Live In Happiness...or...To Die In Search of Happiness."
Your choice.

The End